I'm happy

WAYLAND

Your Feelings

I'm bored   I'm shy
I'm lonely   I'm happy
I'm worried   I feel bullied
It's not fair   I'm special

This edition published in 1999

First published in 1998
by Wayland Publishers Ltd
61 Western Road, Hove
East Sussex BN3 1JD, England

© Copyright 1998 Wayland Publishers Limited

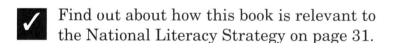

✓ Find out about how this book is relevant to
the National Literacy Strategy on page 31.

Series editor: Alex Woolf
Designer: Malcolm Walker

British Library Cataloguing in Publication Data
Bryant-Mole, Karen
    I'm happy. - (Your feelings)
    1.Happiness - Pictorial works - Juvenile literature
    I.Title
    155.4'12'422

ISBN 0 7502 2396 0

Typeset by Malcolm Walker
Printed and bound in Italy by G. Canale & C.S.p.A., Turin

I'm happy

Written by Karen Bryant-Mole

Illustrated by Mike Gordon

WAYLAND

When I'm feeling happy,
I feel like ...

a bird soaring
through the air ...

the sun, shining warmly ...

a firework exploding
in the night sky.

5

When I'm happy ...

I smile ...

I laugh ...

6

I shout.

When I'm happy ...   I run ...

I jump ...

I just can't keep still.

Being happy is
sometimes noisy.

10

Being happy is sometimes quiet.

When my dad feels happy, he sings.

The dog joins in too!

My mum dances around the living room
when she feels happy.

Grown-ups can be so embarrassing!

There are lots of things that make me feel happy.

16

I feel happy when I find something I have lost.

I feel happy when I go
on holiday.

I feel happy when I come home too.

I feel happy when it's my birthday because everyone is nice to me.

20

Even my sister!

I feel happy when I give
someone a present.

Making other people happy makes
me feel happy too.

I'm not always happy.

When my mum tells me she likes my painting, I feel happy.

But when she tells me to tidy my room,
I feel cross.

I feel happy when I'm playing with my friends.

But when it's time for them
to go home, I feel sad.

Perhaps you know someone who
is not feeling very happy.

What could you
do to help them
feel happy?

Notes for parents and teachers

This book can be read either with individual children or with a group of children. Ask the children to look again at the images on pages 4 and 5 and say which image matches the way they feel when they are feeling happy. See if children can come up with other images that illustrate how they feel. This can be facilitated by encouraging children to start with the phrase, 'I'm as happy as ...'.

Children could think of other words that we use to express the feeling of being happy, such as 'cheerful', 'cheery', 'joyful', 'glad', 'delighted', 'thrilled', 'overjoyed'. We also use phrases to describe happiness, such as 'over the moon', 'on top of the world', 'on cloud nine', 'full of the joys of spring'.

Happiness is often associated with singing. Combine the two and find songs that are about happiness, such as 'If you're happy and you know it clap your hands'. Music itself can sound happy or sad. Play the children different pieces of music and encourage them to describe how it makes them feel.

Many fairy stories end with the words 'and they lived happily ever after'. Children could make up their own stories that end with this phrase. It doesn't have to be a prince and a princess, of course; it could be anything from a family of monsters to a giant and a mouse.

We use the word 'happy' when we wish people well. We say 'Happy Birthday' and 'Happy New Year'. Children could design cards for various occasions that bear the slogan 'Happy' something. As well as the more usual ideas they could include, for example, 'Happy Holidays' or 'Happy Halloween'.

Ask children what makes them feel happy. Encourage them to think beyond the more obvious answers, such as being given presents, to less concrete ideas, such as 'a sunny day' or 'my friend smiling at me'.

Use this book for teaching literacy

This book can help in you in the literacy hour in the following ways:

✓ Children can write simple stories linked to personal experience, using the language of the text in this book as a model for their own writing. (Year 1, Term 3: Non-fiction writing composition)

✓ The repeated use of phrases such as 'When I'm happy ...' or 'I feel happy when ...' helps with word recognition and spelling. (Year 2: Word recognition and graphic knowledge)

✓ Use of speech bubbles and enlarged print shows different ways of presenting texts (Year 2, Term 2: Sentence construction and punctuation)

Books to read

There are many different types of books that relate to happiness. These include books about happy people:

Mrs Jolly's Joke Shop written by Allan Ahlberg, illustrated by Colin McNaughton (Puffin, 1988). This book forms part of the *Happy Families* series. It tells the tale of daily life in the Jolly household and is liberally punctuated with amusing jokes.

The Jolly Witch written by Dick King-Smith, illustrated by Frank Rogers (Simon & Schuster Young Books, 1990; big book edition by Macdonald Young Books, 1997). Mrs Jolly is a school caretaker by day and a witch by night. The story tells the tale of the cheerful Mrs Jolly as she competes in the annual Great Witches' Steeplechase.

There are books about feeling happy, such as:

What Makes Me Happy by Catherine and Laurence Anholt (Walker Books, 1996). This book looks at a variety of emotions by asking what, for instance, makes children laugh or cry, or excited or cross. It uses rhyming words and phrases.

And there are the very many books that have stories with happy endings, for instance:

Little Bird by Rod Campbell (Campbell, 1997). Little Bird feels sad because all the other animals can do things that she can't. Elephant can lift heavy things, Snake can slide through grass and Spider can spin a web. Everything turns out well in the end because Little Bird can fly.